GENERATION CODE

I'M A JAVASCRIPT GAMES MAKER:
ADVANCED CODING

Max Wainewright

WAYLAND

www.waylandbooks.co.uk

CONTENTS

 RESPECTING COPYRIGHT

Copyright means the legal ownership of something. You need to think about who owns the images or sound files you are linking to or downloading to your web pages. There shouldn't be any major issues unless you try to make a page available to the public. Do check with an adult to make sure.

An alternative is to find a free to use image or sound file: search for an image or sound, then look for the **Settings** button on the website results page. Click **Advanced Search** then look for **Usage Rights**. On this menu choose **Free to use, share or modify**.

INTRODUCTION

This book will show you how to code exciting new games using JavaScript. JavaScript is used to make web pages more interactive. It can also be used to create online games that will run on both desktops and mobile devices. By the end of this book, you will have learnt loads of great techniques to make you the ultimate JavaScript expert.

You could use a plain **text editor** to create your code.

mygame.html

```
<script>
alert('Press any key to start')
</script>
```

This will work fine but can be quite fiddly, as the software won't give you any help.

The best thing to use for the activities in this book is an offline HTML text editor. This will support you as you type your code, but also give you the opportunity to learn actual JavaScript code.

There are two separate windows that you'll be using. Arrange them so you can see them both at the same time.

Sublime Text

```
<script>
  var score=0;
  var seconds=0;
  function moveIt(){
    score++;
```

The text editor to enter your code.

Keep saving your work in the editor every few minutes.

Web Browser

Score: 10

The browser to view the program running.

↻ Reload your page to see the changes in your code.

There are many different web browsers you can use. We recommend using Google Chrome for the activities in this book. Make sure you have the latest version installed on your computer before you start.

You will learn some HTML, as well as JavaScript, in this book. HTML is the language used to build web pages. JavaScript is the language that brings those pages to life!

If you would like to learn more about how HTML works, or if you need a beginner's guide to JavaScript, then try reading some of the other books in the *Generation Code* series. But, if you haven't used HTML or JavaScript before, you'll still be able to create all the games in this book.

So what are you waiting for? Get coding!

GETTING STARTED

You need a text editor to start coding in JavaScript. There will probably be a simple text editor already on your computer, called Notepad (if you have Windows), or TextEdit (on a Mac). This will be sufficient for you to get started, but it will be much easier to create JavaScript if you download a more powerful text editor. In this book, we will use a text editor called Sublime Text. There are many others you could download, such as Brackets or Notepad++ – all of these are free for you to try out.

STEP 1 – FIND THE SUBLIME TEXT WEBSITE

⇨ Open your web browser and visit **www.sublimetext.com**

www.sublimetext.com

STEP 2 – START DOWNLOADING

⇨ Click the **Download** button near the top of the web page.

⇨ Choose which version of Sublime Text you need. If you are not sure, then ask an adult to help you find the correct version: click the **Apple** menu, then **About** if you are using a Mac. On a PC, click the **Start** menu, select **System**, and click **About**.

⇨ Wait for the download to complete.

Download

- OSX
- Windows
- Windows 64

STEP 3 – INSTALL THE SOFTWARE

⇨ Some web browsers will then ask you to run the installation program. Choose **Run**.

⇨ If this does not happen, don't panic. The installer file should have been downloaded to your computer. Look in your **Downloads** folder for it. Double-click it to start installing your new text editor. You should get a big white or grey box giving you instructions on what to do next. Follow these instructions to complete the installation.

STEP 4 – RUNNING SUBLIME TEXT

On a PC:

⇨ Click **Start > Programs > Sublime Text.** Or just click **Sublime Text** if it appears in the **Recently added** section.

On a Mac:

⇨ Click **Finder**.

⇨ Click **Applications.**

Applications

⇨ Make a shortcut by dragging **Sublime Text** from **Finder** on to your dock at the bottom of the **Desktop**.

⇨ Click the **Sublime Text** icon.

STEP 5 – START CODING!

⇨ Carefully type this code into lines 1, 2 and 3 of your text editor.

Sublime Text

```
1  <script>
2      alert("Start Coding!")
3  </script>
```

Mark the start of a JavaScript section.

Show a message box saying 'Start Coding!'.

Mark the end of the JavaScript section.

STEP 6 – SAVE YOUR CODE

⇨ Click **File > Save**.

⇨ Save to your **Documents** folder.

⇨ Type **start.html** as the filename.

STEP 7 – VIEW YOUR PAGE

⇨ Open your **Documents** folder.

⇨ Find the **start.html** file and double-click it.

⇨ Your web page should now load in your normal web browser.

⇨ You should get a message saying **Start Coding!**

Documents/start.html

Start Coding!

OK

JAVASCRIPT NEEDS HTML

Although we are coding with JavaScript, we need to put our file inside some HTML code to make it work. HTML stands for HyperText Markup Language and is the language used to build web pages.

HTML is used to describe what objects, or elements. are shown on a web page. If you are creating a simple game, you need to use HTML to add an image and some text to show the score. JavaScript is added to tell the image to move around when different keys are pressed, or the mouse is clicked. It can also be used to display the score and make it change.

We need to use both HTML and JavaScript to make a more interesting game. JavaScript was designed to be added to HTML pages to make them more interactive.

You will use a range of HTML elements in this book. Each element uses tags to show what type of element it is (see page 31). Tags are enclosed with < > angle brackets.

＞UFO POWER UP

In this game, the player has to move an alien spaceship (a UFO) as quickly as possible to get more energy. The player moves the UFO by pressing the arrow keys on the keyboard. The symbol for an atom (in green below) is used to represent the energy source. After the player has completed the task five times, the game stops and the time taken is shown. You can play the game against your friends and see who can complete it in the fastest time! The complete code for the game is listed on page 11.

STEP I – PLANNING

The score is shown in an HTML paragraph element.

A timer will count how long it takes to collect five atoms.

Every time the UFO moves, we need to check if it has reached the atom. This is done by comparing their co-ordinates.

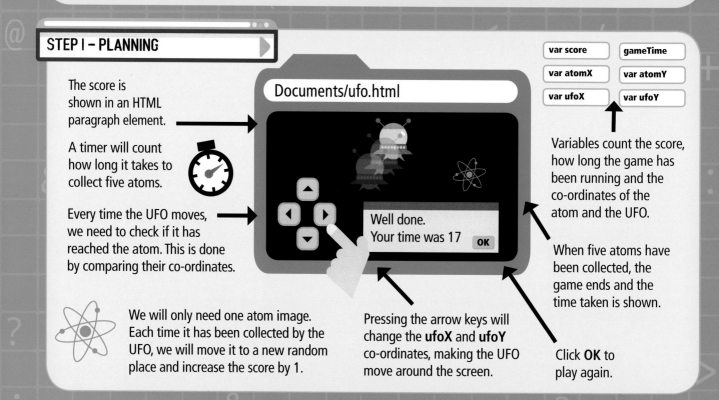

Documents/ufo.html

Well done.
Your time was 17   OK

var score	gameTime
var atomX	var atomY
var ufoX	var ufoY

Variables count the score, how long the game has been running and the co-ordinates of the atom and the UFO.

When five atoms have been collected, the game ends and the time taken is shown.

We will only need one atom image. Each time it has been collected by the UFO, we will move it to a new random place and increase the score by 1.

Pressing the arrow keys will change the **ufoX** and **ufoY** co-ordinates, making the UFO move around the screen.

Click **OK** to play again.

STEP 2 – FIND SOME PICTURES

⇨ Find an image of an atom to use, or find another symbol to represent energy in your game. It needs to be saved into the same folder as your HTML file.

atom clipart   search

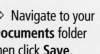

⇨ Search for **atom clipart** to use.

⇨ Right-click one image.

⇨ Click **Save Image As...**

⇨ Navigate to your **Documents** folder then click **Save**.

⇨ Now repeat this step but search for **ufo clipart** to use.

SMOOTH ANIMATIONS

We will add a transition property to the image to make it move smoothly. This means that the image's style properties (i.e. how far it is from the left or top of the screen) will change gradually over a specific amount of time.

All of the style properties will be affected.

`-webkit-transition: all 0.5s;`

The changes will be spread over 0.5 seconds (half a second).

STEP 3 – START A NEW FILE

⇨ Start by typing in the HTML for the game, setting out the body, image and a paragraph for the score.

Sublime Text

```
1  <html>
2  <body style="background-color:black">
3      <img id="atom" style="width: 50px; position:absolute" src="atom.png">
4      <img id="ufo" style="width: 50px; position:absolute; top:0; left:0;
   -webkit-transition: all 0.2s;" src="ufo.png">
5      <p id="scoreTB" style="position:absolute; color:white;">Score: 0</p>
6      <p id="timeTB" style="position:absolute; right:50px; color:white;"
   >Time: 0</p>
7  </body>
```

Set the background colour.

Add the image of the atom. Make sure the src property matches the name of the downloaded file.

Add the ufo image.

Add the score paragraph.

Add the time paragraph.

⇨ Click **File > Save** and type **ufo.html** as the filename.

⇨ Make sure you save it in your **Documents** folder. Keep saving it every few minutes.

STEP 4 – BEGIN THE SCRIPT

Now that we have defined the elements that go on the page, we need to start on the JavaScript.
At the start of the game we need to:

- create the variables
- define a function to make random numbers
- tell the program which function to run when the page is loaded and ready.
- tell the program which function to run when keys are pressed
- define some functions to set co-ordinates

```
8   <script>
9       var score=0, gameTime=0, gameTimer, ufoX=0, ufoY=0, atomX=0, atomY=0;
10      onkeydown=handleKeys;
11      onready=startUp();
12      function setLeft(id,x){document.getElementById(id).style.left=x+"px";}
13      function setTop(id,y){document.getElementById(id).style.top=y+"px";}
14      function randomNumber(low,high){return(Math.floor(low+Math.
    random()*(1+high-low)));}
```

Start the script section.

Create variables to store the score, gameTime and co-ordinates.

Tell the program which function to run when keys are pressed.

Tell the program which function to run when the page is ready.

Define functions to set any element's co-ordinates.

Define a function that returns a random number between two values.

STEP 5 – GET STARTED

⇨ Once the page has loaded in the browser, the **startUp** function will be called. ('Calling' a function means running it and carrying out all the code inside it.) The **startUp** function will run code to move the atom icon to a random place and the game timer will be started.

15	`function startUp(){`	Define the function.
16	`    moveAtom();`	Call the moveAtom function.
17	`    gameTimer=window.setInterval(displayTime, 1000);`	Start the gameTimer. This timer will call the function named displayTime every 1000 milliseconds (every second).
18	`}`	End the function.

STEP 6 – HOW LONG?

⇨ Add the **displayTime** variable. This will store how many seconds the game has been running.

19	`function displayTime(){`	Define the function.
20	`    gameTime++;`	Add one to the value stored in the gameTime variable.
21	`    document.getElementById("timeTB").innerText="Time:"+gameTime;`	Show the time left in the paragraph called timeTB.
22	`}`	End the function.

POSITIONING ELEMENTS

Documents/ufo.html

(0,0) left →

(100,50)

top ↓

Computer images are made up of pixels (picture elements). Pixels can be used as units for co-ordinates in JavaScript and HTML.

Elements can be positioned in a particular place by setting their co-ordinates. This is done by setting their left and top style properties. Add **px** on the end of the value to measure in pixels.

(0,0) will always be the co-ordinates for the top left of the browser. The maximum values for left and top will depend on the size of the browser window. The co-ordinates of the red dot on this screen are (100,50).

STEP 7 – MOVE THE ATOM

⇨ We need to define a function that will move the atom to a random place on the screen.

23	`function moveAtom(){`	Define the function.
24	`atomX=randomNumber(2,16);`	Set atomX to a random number between 2 and 16.
25	`atomY=randomNumber(2,16);`	Set atomY to a random number between 2 and 16.
26	`setLeft("atom",50*atomX);`	Set the new position for the atom symbol by multiplying atomX by 50 and atomY by 50 (* means multiply, and is used in JavaScript instead of the mathematical symbol x).
27	`setTop("atom",50*atomY);`	
28	`}`	

STEP 8 – MOVE THE UFO

⇨ When the arrow keys are pressed, we need to move the UFO up, down, left or right – which direction depends on which key is pressed. We need to add a special sort of variable called a parameter to our function, which will store the information about the key that has been pressed. Type **(e)** after the function name to add the parameter.

Each key on the keyboard has a specific code linked to it. The left arrow has a code of 37, the right arrow's code is 39, up is 38 and down is 40. The code for the key pressed will be stored in **e.keyCode**. Type in this function to trigger what will happen when a key is pressed:

29	`function handleKeys(e){`	Define a function called handleKeys. Information about which key is pressed will be put into the variable called **e**.
30	`if(e.keyCode==37){ufoX--;}`	If the code for the left arrow key has been sent, make ufoX go down by 1. (ufoX-- means subtract one from the value in ufoX.)
31	`if(e.keyCode==39){ufoX++;}`	If the code for the right arrow key has been sent, make ufoX go up by 1. (ufoX++ means add 1 to ufoX.)
32	`if(e.keyCode==38){ufoY--;}`	If the up arrow key has been pressed, subtract 1 from ufoY.
33	`if(e.keyCode==40){ufoY++;}`	If the down arrow key has been pressed, add 1 to ufoY.
34	`setLeft("ufo",50*ufoX);`	Set the new position for the UFO by multiplying ufoX by 50 and ufoY by 50.
35	`setTop("ufo",50*ufoY);`	
36	`checkIfHitAtom();`	Once the UFO has moved, we will need to check if it has hit the atom symbol by running the checkIfHitAtom() function.
37	`}`	

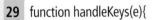

Remember, events are special bits of code that 'listen' to the mouse or keyboard and wait for certain things to happen before running some other code.

STEP 9 – HIT OR MISS?

⇨ Every time the UFO moves, it calls the function below. This function will check to see if the UFO has hit the atom symbol. We code this by comparing the **x** co-ordinates (how far from the left) and **y** co-ordinates (how far from the top) of the atom and UFO. If they are equal then they both must be in the same position. Therefore, the UFO has hit the atom symbol and topped up its energy levels!

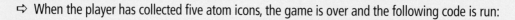

38 `function checkIfHitAtom(){`	
39 `  if((ufoX==atomX) && (ufoY==atomY)){`	If the co-ordinates match, run the code below (&& means and).
40 `    score++;`	Increase the score by 1.
41 `    document.getElementById("scoreTB").innerText="Score: "+score;`	Show the score in the paragraph called scoreTB.
42 `    moveAtom();`	Move the atom symbol to a new random place.
43 `    if(score==5){gameOver();}`	If the score gets up to 5 then the player has won, so call the gameOver function.
44 `  }`	
45 `}`	

STEP 10 – GAME OVER

⇨ When the player has collected five atom icons, the game is over and the following code is run:

46 `function gameOver(){`	Define the function.
47 `  clearInterval(gameTimer);`	Stop the timer running, so the time won't keep going up.
48 `  alert("Well done! Your time was: "+ gameTime);`	Show a message explaining how long the player took to complete the game.
49 `  location.reload();`	This command will reload the page and make the game start again. (If you don't want this to happen, miss out this line.)
50 `}`	

STEP 11 – LAST LINES

⇨ Finally, add these two lines to show the end of the script section and the end of the HTML.

```
51 </script>
52 </html>
```

 Save your file, reload the browser, then play!

CUSTOMISE

• Change the game so the player has to collect 10 atom icons.

• Design your own collecting game using different images.

THE COMPLETE CODE

```
1    <html>
2    <body style="background-color:black">
3        <img id="atom" style="width: 50px; position:absolute" src="atom.png">
4        <img id="ufo" style="width: 50px; position:absolute; top:0; left:0; -webkit-
     transition: all 0.2s;" src="ufo.png">
5        <p id="scoreTB" style="position:absolute; color:white;">Score: 0</p>
6        <p id="timeTB" style="position:absolute; right:50px; color:white;">Time: 0</p>
7    </body>
8    <script>
9        var score=0, gameTime=0, gameTimer, ufoX=0, ufoY=0, atomX=0, atomY=0;
10       onkeydown=handleKeys;
11       onready=startUp();
12       function setLeft(id,x){document.getElementById(id).style.left=x+"px";}
13       function setTop(id,y){document.getElementById(id).style.top=y+"px";}
14       function randomNumber(low,hi){return (Math.floor(low+Math.random()*(1+hi-low)));}
15       function startUp(){
16           moveAtom();
17           gameTimer=window.setInterval(displayTime, 1000);
18       }
19       function displayTime(){
20           gameTime++;
21           document.getElementById("timeTB").innerText="Time: "+gameTime;
22       }
23       function moveAtom(){
24           atomX=randomNumber(2,16);
25           atomY=randomNumber(2,16);
26           setLeft("atom",50*atomX);
27           setTop("atom",50*atomY);
28       }
29       function handleKeys(e){
30           if(e.keyCode==37){ufoX--;}
31           if(e.keyCode==39){ufoX++;}
32           if(e.keyCode==38){ufoY--;}
33           if(e.keyCode==40){ufoY++;}
34           setLeft("ufo",50*ufoX);
35           setTop("ufo",50*ufoY);
36           checkIfHitAtom();
37       }
38       function checkIfHitAtom(){
39           if((ufoX==atomX) && (ufoY==atomY)){
40               score++;
41               document.getElementById("scoreTB").innerText="Score:"+score;
42               moveAtom();
43               if(score==5){gameOver();}
44           }
45       }
46       function gameOver(){
47           clearInterval(gameTimer);
48           alert("Well done! Your time was:"+gameTime);
49           location.reload();
50       }
51   </script>
52   </html>
```

›GHOST MAZE

In this project, you will make a simple maze game. The player will move around when the arrow keys are pressed. To stop the player moving through walls, we will store the maze shape in a special data structure. This is called a two-dimensional array, which is a list of lists that stores which squares in the maze are walls and which squares aren't. Finally, we will check to see where the player is and show a message when they reach the exit of the maze. The complete code for the game is listed on page 17.

STEP 1 – PLANNING

A grid of data is used to draw the maze when the game starts. Walls will be drawn in yellow and paths in blue.

Before the player is allowed to move, we need to check that it is not going to hit a wall. This is done by checking **mazeData**.

Pressing the arrow keys will change the player icon's co-ordinates, making it move around the screen.

Documents/maze.html

Well done!

OK

Every time the player moves, we need to check if it has reached the exit. This is done by checking co-ordinates.

`var mazeData`

The maze information is stored as ones and zeros. 1 means a wall, 0 means a path.

`var px`   `var py`

Variables store the co-ordinates of the player.

Show a message at the exit.

STEP 2 – FIND A PICTURE

⇨ First of all, you need to find an image to use. It needs to be placed in the same folder as your HTML file.

`ghost clipart`   `search`

⇨ Go online and search for some clipart to use.

⇨ Right-click one image.

⇨ Click **Save Image As...**

⇨ Navigate to your **Documents** folder then click **Save**.

⇨ Start by typing in the HTML for the game. Add code for the body, maze holder and player (the ghost, which will move around when we play the game). The maze will be built later, but we need to prepare a special container to hold the blocks in – the **mazeHolder**. We will also add a special style section that will contain the size and colour of each of the maze blocks.

Sublime Text

```
1  <html>
2  <body style="background-color:black">
3      <div id="mazeHolder" style="position:absolute; top:0; left:0;"></div>
4      <img id="player" style="position:absolute; width:50px; top:50px; left:0;
   -webkit-transition: all 0.2s;" src="ghost.png" >
5      <style>
6          div{position:absolute; background-color:yellow; width:50px;
   height:50px;}
7      </style>
8  </body>
```

Set the background colour.

Create a box to hold all the blocks for the maze.

Match the src property to the name of the downloaded file.

Start the style section.

This styles the div elements that will make up blocks in the maze.

End the style section.

⇨ Click **File** > **Save** and type **maze.html** as the filename.

⇨ Make sure you save it in your **Documents** folder. Keep saving it every few minutes.

THE MAZE DATA

When developers design a game that has a maze, or some walls or platforms, they need to find a way to make sure the objects in the game stop when they hit something hard. There are lots of ways of doing this, but all involve some kind of data structure that keeps information about where the hard objects are. In this game, we will create a special grid of data called a 2D array, which uses ones and zeros to represent the walls and paths.

```
var mazeData=[
    [1,1,1,1,1,1,1,1],
    [0,0,1,1,0,0,0,1],
    [1,0,0,0,0,1,1,1],
    [1,0,1,1,0,1,0,1],
    [1,0,1,1,0,0,0,1],
    [1,0,0,0,0,1,0,0],
    [1,1,1,1,1,1,1,1]
];
```

We need to turn the ones into yellow walls. They may look a little orange in colour when viewed on the web page.

All the zeros need to be turned into blue paths.

The colour we choose to draw the maze in won't matter. What will matter is all the ones and zeros. We will use these to stop the player walking through the walls.

STEP 5 – ENTER THE MAZE DATA

⇨ Start the script section and enter the maze data.
Create an array called **mazeData** to store it in as a 2D array.

9	`<script>`	Start the script section.
10	`var mazeData=[`	Create the mazeData array.
11	`[1,1,1,1,1,1,1,1],`	Type in the data very carefully. Each row of the maze becomes a list within the array. Each square in the maze is 0 or 1 and is separated by a comma. Each list must start and end with a square bracket [ ]. Once you have the code running you can try changing this data to change the layout of the maze.
12	`[0,0,1,1,0,0,0,1],`	
13	`[1,0,0,0,0,1,1,1],`	
14	`[1,0,1,1,0,1,0,1],`	
15	`[1,0,1,1,0,0,0,1],`	
16	`[1,0,0,0,0,1,0,0],`	
17	`[1,1,1,1,1,1,1,1]`	
18	`];`	End the mazeData array.

STEP 6 – VARIABLES AND SIMPLE FUNCTIONS

⇨ Type in the code that tells the program what to do when keys are pressed and the program starts up.
Create the variables you need and define the functions to set co-ordinates.

19	`onkeydown=handleKeys;`	When any keys are pressed, call the function named handleKeys.
20	`onready=drawMaze();`	When the page has loaded, call the function named drawMaze.
21	`var px=0, py=1;`	Create the co-ordinate variables.
22	`function setLeft(id,x){document.getElementById(id).style.left=x+"px";}`	Define functions to set any element's co-ordinates.
23	`function setTop(id,y){document.getElementById(id).style.top=y+"px";}`	

STEP 7 – DRAW THE MAZE

⇨ The maze needs to be drawn on the page using the infomation in the **mazeData** array. The function below will loop through the array and create a **div** element for each square in the maze. It will then look at whether the relevant item in the maze data is a 0 or 1. If it is a 1 it will leave the **div** yellow, if it is 0 then it will colour it blue.

24	`function drawMaze(){`	
25	`  for(var y=0; y<7; y++){`	Loop through each row of the maze.
26	`    for(var x=0; x<8; x++){`	Loop through each column of the maze.
27	`      var newOb=document.createElement('div');`	Create a new div called newOb.
28	`      document.getElementById("mazeHolder").appendChild(newOb);`	Add it to the mazeHolder.
29	`      var divId=Math.random();`	The div needs a name. Make up a random one!
30	`      newOb.setAttribute('id',divId);`	Teach the div its new name.
31	`      setLeft(divId,50*x);`	Position it on the mazeHolder in the correct place based on its co-ordinates. The **x** and **y** values are multiplied (*) by 50 as each block is 50 x 50 pixels.
32	`      setTop(divId,50*y);`	
33	`      if(mazeData[y][x]==0){`	If the relevant item in mazeData is 0 then:
34	`        document.getElementById(divId).style.backgroundColor="blue";`	Colour the div blue to make it a path.
35	`      }`	End the IF command block.
36	`    }`	End the **x** loop.
37	`  }`	End the **y** loop.
38	`}`	End the function.

STEP 8 – MOVE THE PLAYER

⇨ When the arrow keys are pressed, we need to move the player up, down, left or right. However, we also need to check to see if moving the player will make it bump into a wall. To do this, we need to look at the value in the **mazeData** item the player is going to move into. If it is 0 then the player will be allowed to move. If it is 1 then the player would hit a wall, so the player cannot move.

39	`function handleKeys(e){`	Define a function called handleKeys.
40	`  if((e.keyCode==37)&&mazeData[py][px-1]==0){px--;}`	If the left arrow key is pressed and there is no wall to the left of the player, subtract 1 from px.
41	`  if((e.keyCode==39)&&mazeData[py][px+1]==0){px++;}`	If the right arrow key is pressed and there is no wall to the right of the player, add 1 to px.
42	`  if((e.keyCode==38)&&mazeData[py-1][px]==0){py--;}`	If the up or down arrow is pressed and the player won't hit a wall if it moves, then change py in the same way.
43	`  if((e.keyCode==40)&&mazeData[py+1][px]==0){py++;}`	
44	`  setLeft("player",px*50);`	Set the new position for the player by multiplying px by 50 and py by 50.
45	`  setTop("player",py*50);`	
46	`  if(px==7 && py==5){alert("Well done!");}`	If px and py match the co-ordinates of the exit then show a message saying 'Well done!'.
47	`}`	

STEP 9 – FINISH THE GAME

⇨ Finally, add these two lines to show the end of the script section and the end of the HTML.

```
48 </script>
49 </html>
```

Save your file, reload the browser then test your maze!

GRAPHICS STORED AS DATA

Instead of using a background picture, information about the game world is stored in a 2D array – a list of lists.

DYNAMIC ELEMENTS

So far we have added elements to the page by typing in HTML, but sometimes there are too many elements to add in this way. We may want to set details, such as what colour an element is or when a program runs. An element created when JavaScript runs is called a dynamic element.

CUSTOMISE

•Experiment with a different maze layout by changing some of the 1s and 0s in **mazeData.**

•Make a much larger maze and try using different colours.

1. Start by planning your maze on some squared paper. Make sure it can be solved!

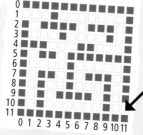

2. Change your maze into ones and zeros. Use 1 when you want a wall. Replace lines 10 to 18 of your original code with your new data.

```
var mazeData=[
    [1,1,1,1,1,1,1,1,1,1,1,1],
    [0,0,0,1,0,0,0,0,0,0,0,1],
    [1,0,1,1,1,1,0,1,1,1,0,1],
    [1,0,0,0,1,0,0,0,0,1,0,1],
    [1,1,1,0,0,0,1,1,0,0,0,1],
    [1,0,1,1,0,1,1,1,1,1,1,1],
    [1,0,0,0,0,1,0,0,0,0,0,1],
    [1,0,1,1,0,1,0,1,1,1,0,1],
    [1,0,1,0,0,1,0,0,0,1,0,1],
    [1,0,1,0,1,1,1,1,0,1,0,1],
    [1,0,1,0,0,0,0,0,0,1,0,0],
    [1,1,1,1,1,1,1,1,1,1,1,1],
];
```

3. In the **drawMaze** function you will need to change how many times the loops run. In the example shown, both need to be changed to 12, because the maze is 12 columns wide and 12 rows deep (the co-ordinates start from 0).

4. Set the co-ordinates for the position of the new exit. (In the example, this would be px==11 and py==10).

`if(px==7 && py==5){alert("Well done!");}`

Change 7 to the number of rows in your new maze.

↓

`for(var y=0; y<7; y++) {`

`for(var x=0; x<8; x++){`

↑

Change 8 to the number of columns in your new maze.

THE COMPLETE CODE

```
1    <html>
2    <body style="background-color:black">
3       <div id="mazeHolder" style="position:absolute; top:0; left:0;"></div>
4       <img id="player" style="position:absolute; width:50px; top:50px; left:0; -webkit-transition:
     all 0.2s;" src="ghost.png" >
5       <style>
6          div{position:absolute; background-color:yellow; width:50px; height:50px;}
7       </style>
8    </body>
9    <script>
10      var mazeData=[
11         [1,1,1,1,1,1,1,1],
12         [0,0,1,1,0,0,0,1],
13         [1,0,0,0,0,1,1,1],
14         [1,0,1,1,0,1,0,1],
15         [1,0,1,1,0,0,0,1],
16         [1,0,0,0,0,1,0,0],
17         [1,1,1,1,1,1,1,1]
18      ];
19      onkeydown=handleKeys;
20      onready=drawMaze();
21      var px=0, py=1;
22      function setLeft(id,x){document.getElementById(id).style.left=x+"px";}
23      function setTop(id,y){document.getElementById(id).style.top=y+"px";}
24      function drawMaze(){
25         for(var y=0; y<7; y++){
26            for(var x=0; x<8; x++){
27               var newOb=document.createElement('div');
28               document.getElementById("mazeHolder").appendChild(newOb);
29               var divId=Math.random();
30               newOb.setAttribute('id',divId);
31               setLeft(divId,50*x);
32               setTop(divId,50*y);
33               if(mazeData[y][x]==0){
34                document.getElementById(divId).style.backgroundColor="blue";
35               }
36            }
37         }
38      }
39      function handleKeys(e){
40         if((e.keyCode==37)&&mazeData[py][px-1]==0){px--;}
41         if((e.keyCode==39)&&mazeData[py][px+1]==0){px++;}
42         if((e.keyCode==38)&&mazeData[py-1][px]==0){py--;}
43         if((e.keyCode==40)&&mazeData[py+1][px]==0){py++;}
44         setLeft("player",px*50);
45         setTop("player",py*50);
46         if(px==7 && py==5){alert("Well done!");}
47      }
48   </script>
49   </html>
```

❯ ROCK STORM

This game is a simple side scrolling game: rocks will move across the screen from the right, towards a spaceship, controlled by the player. Pressing the **up** and **down** arrows will allow the spaceship to avoid the rocks. Each time the rocks move, a function will check if they have hit the spaceship. The score will be stored in a variable, and will increase each time the spaceship avoids a rock. When you play the game, maximise your screen so the game is bigger and it is easy to avoid the rocks. The complete code for the game is listed on page 23.

STEP 1 – PLANNING

The score is shown in an HTML paragraph element **<p>**.

Pressing the **up** and **down** arrow keys will make the spaceship move up and down the screen.

A timer will move the rocks every 20 milliseconds.

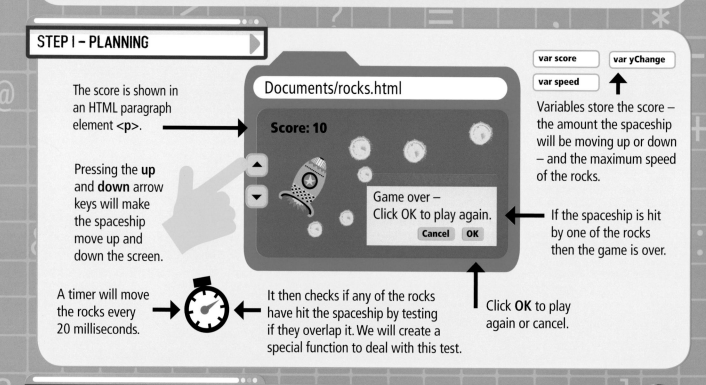

Documents/rocks.html

Score: 10

Game over –
Click OK to play again.

Cancel   OK

It then checks if any of the rocks have hit the spaceship by testing if they overlap it. We will create a special function to deal with this test.

var score   var yChange

var speed

Variables store the score – the amount the spaceship will be moving up or down – and the maximum speed of the rocks.

If the spaceship is hit by one of the rocks then the game is over.

Click **OK** to play again or cancel.

STEP 2 – FIND SOME IMAGES

⇨ Find an image of a spaceship to use. It needs to be saved into the same folder as your HTML file.

⇨ Search the internet for spaceship clipart to use.

⇨ Right-click one image.

⇨ Click **Save Image As...**

⇨ Navigate to your **Documents** folder then click **Save**.

⇨ Now repeat this step but search for **space rock clipart** to use.

⇨ Start by typing in the HTML for the game. Add code for the body, four images and a paragraph for the score.

Sublime Text

```
1  <html>
2  <body style="background-color:#8060AA">
3     <img id="ship" style="position:absolute; width:100px; left:50px;"
   src="spcshp.png">
4     <img id="rock1" style="position:absolute; width:100px; left:-200px;"
   src="rock.png">
5     <img id="rock2" style="position:absolute; width:100px; left:-200px;"
   src="rock.png">
6     <img id="rock3" style="position:absolute; width:100px; left:-200px;"
   src="rock.png">
7     <p id="scoreTB" style="position:absolute; color:yellow; font-size:20px;
   font-family:Arial">Score: 0</p>
8  </body>
```

Set the background colour.

Make sure the src property matches the name of the downloaded file for the spaceship.

Add code for the three rocks. The code for each is very similar, but the ID for each is different – rock1, rock2 and rock3. Make sure the src property is correct.

Add the score paragraph.

⇨ Click **File** > **Save** and type **rocks.html** as the filename.

⇨ Make sure you save it in your **Documents** folder. Keep saving it every time you add any code.

> Setting co-ordinates means moving an element to a new place on the screen. Getting co-ordinates means finding out where an element is.

At the start of the script we need to:

- create the variables we need
- tell the program which function to run when keys are pressed
- tell the program which function to run when the page has been loaded and is ready
- define a function to make random numbers
- define some functions to get and set co-ordinates.

```
9   <script>
10    var score=0, yChange=3, speed=5, gameTimer;
11    document.onkeydown=handleKeys;
12    onready=startUp();
13    function setLeft(id,x){document.getElementById(id).style.left=x+"px";}
14    function setTop(id,y){document.getElementById(id).style.top=y+"px";}
15    function getLeft(id){return document.getElementById(id).offsetLeft;}
16    function getTop(id){return document.getElementById(id).offsetTop;}
17    function randomNumber(low,high){return(Math.floor(low+Math.
   random()*(1+high-low)));}
```

Start the script section.

Create required variables.

Run this function when keys are pressed.

Run this function when the page is ready.

Define functions to set any element's co-ordinates.

Define functions to get any element's co-ordinates.

Define a function that returns a random number between two values.

HIT OR OVERLAPPING?

In the previous two games, we moved objects by 50 or 100 pixels at a time. This made it easy to see if objects had hit each other, after testing the **x** (how far from the left) and **y** (how far from the top) co-ordinates. In a game where objects move by smaller amounts, they may hit each other, but not have exactly the same co-ordinates. To test for this, we need to see if the two objects are overlapping.

(50, 85)

(120, 140)

Both of these objects are 100 pixels wide and 100 pixels high.

We know these objects are overlapping, because the difference between their left values is less than their width:

120-50=70

And the difference between their top values is less than their height:

140-85=55

This means they are overlapping and have collided.

STEP 6 – OVERLAPPING TEST CODE ▶

⇨ We need a function that can test if any of the three rocks are overlapping the ship. Rather than write separate code for each rock, we will write a function that can test if any two objects are overlapping. We will call these two imaginary objects **ob1** and **ob2**. When we call the function, we will tell it which two objects we want to use in the overlapping test.

```
18  function isOverlapping(ob1,ob2){

19      return ((getLeft(ob1)+100>getLeft(ob2))
     && (getLeft(ob1)<getLeft(ob2)+100) &&
     (getTop(ob1)+100>getTop(ob2)) &&
     (getTop(ob1)<getTop(ob2)+100));}
```

Add the code that returns (sends back) a value after testing co-ordinates of the two objects. It returns true if the objects are overlapping, or false if they are not. It assumes the objects are 100 pixels high and 100 pixels wide.

STEP 7 – START UP ▶

⇨ Once the page has loaded in the browser the **startUp** function will be called. The **startUp** function will set up a timer to move the rocks.

```
20  function startUp(){

21      gameTimer=window.setInterval(moveThings,20);

22  }
```

Start the gameTimer. This timer will call the function named moveThings every 20 milliseconds (50 times a second).

⇨ All three rocks need to move when the timer calls the **moveThings** function. We could do this by writing a section of code to move **rock1**, another to move **rock2** and a final section to move **rock3**. But this would require a lot of code and would mean we would need to change each section if we wanted to make the rocks faster or slower. Instead, we will use a loop to move each of the rocks in turn and check if it has hit the spaceship. Our loop will count from 1 to 3. The first time it will move **rock1**, then **rock2** and then **rock3**. To do this, we need to write a general bit of code that will move an imaginary rock, called **rock n**. We can give **n** a value between 1 and 3. This will be written as **"rock"+n**.

⇨ Finally, we need to move the spaceship up or down. To make the game harder, the spaceship won't keep still.

23	`function moveThings(){`	
24	`for(var n=1; n<=3; n++){`	Start a loop that runs from 1 to 3.
25	`var x=getLeft("rock"+n);`	Get the **x** co-ordinate of the first rock.
26	`if(x<-100){`	If it has moved beyond the screen edge then run this code:
27	`x=window.innerWidth;`	Move it to the screen edge on the right.
28	`y=randomNumber(0,window.innerHeight-100);`	Pick a random value for the variable **y**.
29	`setTop("rock"+n,y);`	Use **y** to set the rock's **y** co-ordinate.
30	`score=score+10;`	Add 10 to the score.
31	`document.getElementById("scoreTB").innerText="Score: "+score;`	Display the score.
32	`}`	End the IF statement.
33	`setLeft("rock"+n,x-speed-n);`	Move the rock to the left. Each rock will have a slightly different speed.
34	`if(isOverlapping("rock"+n,"ship")){`	Test to see if the rock is overlapping the spaceship (have they collided?).
35	`gameOver();`	If so, the game is over.
36	`}`	End the IF statement.
37	`}`	End the loop. The next rock will be moved.
38	`var y=getTop("ship");`	Get the **y** co-ordinate of the spaceship.
39	`if((y<=0) || (y>window.innerHeight-100)){yChange=-yChange;}`	If it has reached the top or bottom, change direction. Two | symbols mean 'or'.
40	`setTop("ship",y+yChange);`	Move the spaceship up or down.
41	`}`	End the function.

STEP 9 – CHANGE DIRECTION

⇨ To make the game harder, the spaceship keeps moving either up or down. Pressing one of the keys will set its direction, but it gets moved in the **moveThings** function. Type in this function to decide what will happen when a key is pressed.

42	`function handleKeys(e){`	Define a function called handleKeys. Information about which key was pressed will be stored in the variable **e**.
43	`if(e.keyCode==38){yChange=-3;}`	If the code for the **up** arrow key has been passed to the function, set yChange to -3.
44	`if(e.keyCode==40){yChange=3;}`	If the code for the down arrow key has been sent, set yChange to 3.
45	`}`	End the function.

STEP 10 – COLLISION

⇨ If one of the rocks hits the spaceship, then the following function will be called:

46	`function gameOver(){`	Define the function.
47	`clearInterval(gameTimer);`	Stop the timer running so the time won't keep going up.
48	`if(confirm("Game Over – Click OK to play again.")==true){`	Show a message asking the player if they want to play again. If they click OK run the next line.
49	`location.reload();`	Reload the page and make the game start again.
50	`}`	End the IF statement.
51	`}`	End the function.

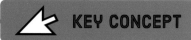

STEP 11 – THE END

⇨ Finally, add these two lines to show the end of the script section and the end of the HTML.

52	`</script>`
53	`</html>`

Save your file, reload the **browser**, then play!

KEY CONCEPT

LOOPING THROUGH ELEMENTS
Use a loop to move a number of objects with similar names, such as **rock1**, **rock2** and **rock3**.

HIT TESTING
Check for collisions using a function that tests if any two particular objects are overlapping.

THE COMPLETE CODE

```html
1    <html>
2    <body style="background-color:#8060AA">
3        <img id="ship" style="position:absolute; width:100px; left:50px;" src="spcshp.png">
4        <img id="rock1" style="position:absolute; width:100px; left:-200px;" src="rock.png">
5        <img id="rock2" style="position:absolute; width:100px; left:-200px;" src="rock.png">
6        <img id="rock3" style="position:absolute; width:100px; left:-200px;" src="rock.png">
7        <p id="scoreTB" style="position:absolute; color:yellow; font-size:20px; font-
     family:Arial">Score: 0</p>
8    </body>
9    <script>
10     var score=0, yChange=3, speed=5, gameTimer;
11     document.onkeydown=handleKeys;
12     onready=startUp();
13     function setLeft(id,x){document.getElementById(id).style.left=x+"px";}
14     function setTop(id,y){document.getElementById(id).style.top=y+"px";}
15     function getLeft(id){return document.getElementById(id).offsetLeft;}
16     function getTop(id){return document.getElementById(id).offsetTop;}
17     function randomNumber(low,high){return (Math.floor(low+Math.random()*(1+high-low)));}
18     function isOverlapping(ob1, ob2){
19       return ((getLeft(ob1)+100>getLeft(ob2)) && (getLeft(ob1)<getLeft(ob2)+100) &&
     (getTop(ob1)+100>getTop(ob2)) && (getTop(ob1)<getTop(ob2)+100));}
20     function startUp(){
21       gameTimer=window.setInterval(moveThings,20);
22     }
23     function moveThings(){
24       for(var n=1; n<=3; n++){
25         var x=getLeft("rock"+n);
26         if(x<-100){
27           x=window.innerWidth;
28           y=randomNumber(0,window.innerHeight-100);
29           setTop("rock"+n,y);
30           score=score+10;
31           document.getElementById("scoreTB").innerText="Score: "+score;
32         }
33         setLeft("rock"+n,x-speed-n);
34         if(isOverlapping("rock"+n,"ship")){
35           gameOver();
36         }
37       }
38       var y=getTop("ship");
39       if((y<=0) || (y>window.innerHeight-100)){yChange=-yChange;}
40       setTop("ship",y+yChange);
41     }
42     function handleKeys(e){
43       if(e.keyCode==38){yChange=-3;}
44       if(e.keyCode==40){yChange=3;}
45     }
46     function gameOver(){
47       clearInterval(gameTimer);
48       if(confirm("Game Over – Click OK to play again.")==true){
49         location.reload();
50       }
51     }
52   </script>
53   </html>
```

CUSTOMISE

• Try and make the game harder by altering the speed of the rocks and the spaceship.

• Add a fourth rock called **rock4**. Alter the loop to make it move.

• Build your own game where the player has to dodge moving objects. It could be set underwater...

❯ SUBMARINE EXPLORER

This game involves the player guiding a submarine around the screen, trying to catch treasure that has fallen overboard from a shipwreck. It uses a different moving system that is often used in things like driving games and side flying games to steer and move at an angle. Some complex maths is used to handle the angles. The game also includes basic sound effects. The complete code for the game is listed on page 29.

STEP 1 – PLANNING

The score is shown in an HTML paragraph element <p>.

A timer will move the coin and the submarine.

Every time the sub moves we need to check if it has grabbed a coin. This is done by using a function to test for overlapping.

If a coin has been caught then a sound effect will play.

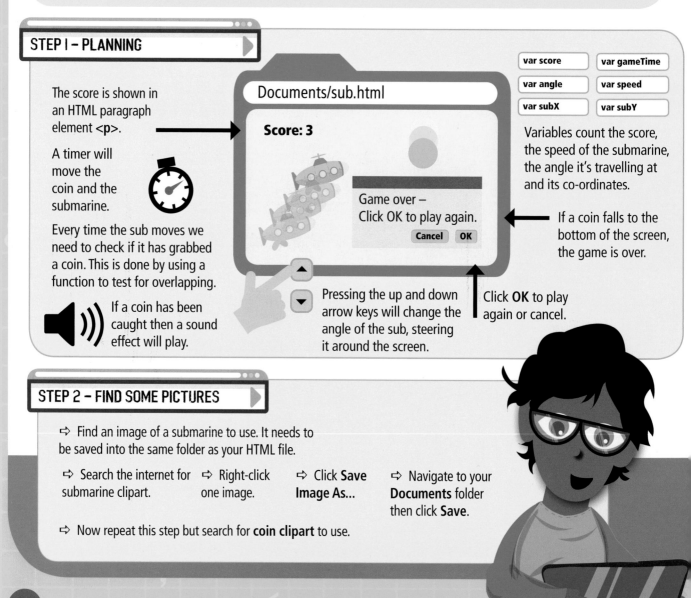

Documents/sub.html

Score: 3

Game over –
Click OK to play again.

Cancel   OK

Pressing the up and down arrow keys will change the angle of the sub, steering it around the screen.

var score	var gameTime
var angle	var speed
var subX	var subY

Variables count the score, the speed of the submarine, the angle it's travelling at and its co-ordinates.

If a coin falls to the bottom of the screen, the game is over.

Click **OK** to play again or cancel.

STEP 2 – FIND SOME PICTURES

⇨ Find an image of a submarine to use. It needs to be saved into the same folder as your HTML file.

⇨ Search the internet for submarine clipart.

⇨ Right-click one image.

⇨ Click **Save Image As...**

⇨ Navigate to your **Documents** folder then click **Save**.

⇨ Now repeat this step but search for **coin clipart** to use.

STEP 3 - SOUND FILE

⇨ We need a sound effect to play when the sub grabs a coin. You may already have some on your computer. If not, search online for a sound file to download and use.

 beep mp3   search

⇨ Every website shown in your results will be different. Try to find one that will let you download mp3 files.

beep.mp3

 Play   Download

STEP 4 - START A NEW FILE

⇨ Start by typing in the HTML for the game. Add code for the body, both images and a paragraph for the score.

Sublime Text

```
1  <html>
2  <body style="background-color:#2980b9">
3      <img id="sub" style="position:absolute; top:500px; width:100px;"
   src="sub.png">
4      <img id="coin" style="position:absolute; left:300px; width: 50px;"
   src="coin.png">
5      <p id="scoreTB" style="position:absolute; color:white; font-size:
   20px; font-family:Arial">Score: 0</p>
6  </body>
```

Set the background colour.

Make sure the src property matches the name of the downloaded file for the submarine.

Make sure the src property matches the downloaded file for the coin.

Add the score paragraph.

STEP 5 - SAVE YOUR CODE

⇨ Click **File** > **Save** and type **sub.html** as the filename.

⇨ Make sure you save it in your **Documents** folder. Keep saving it every time you add some new code.

STEP 6 – BEGIN THE SCRIPT ▶

At the start of the script we need to:

- create the variables we need
- tell the program which function to run when keys are pressed
- start the **gameTimer** and tell it to call the **moveThings** function every 20 milliseconds
- define some functions to get and set co-ordinates, and make random numbers.

7	`<script>`	Start the script section.
8	`var score=0, angle=0, speed=4, subX=0, subY=500, gameTimer;`	Create the variables.
9	`onkeydown=handleKeys;`	When keys are pressed, run function.
10	`gameTimer=window.setInterval(moveThings,20);`	Tell the timer to start running
11	`function setLeft(id,x){document.getElementById(id).style.left=x+"px";}`	Define functions to set any
12	`function setTop(id,y){document.getElementById(id).style.top=y+"px";}`	element's co-ordinates.
13	`function getLeft(id){return document.getElementById(id).offsetLeft;}`	Define functions to get any
14	`function getTop(id){return document.getElementById(id).offsetTop;}`	element's co-ordinates.
15	`function randomNumber(low,high){return(Math.floor(low+Math.random()*(1+high-low)));}`	Define a function that returns a random number between two values.

STEP 7 – OVERLAPPING TEST CODE ▶

⇨ We will use the function used on page 20 to test if objects called **ob1** and **ob2** are overlapping.

16	`function isOverlapping(ob1, ob2){`	Define the function.
17	`return ((getLeft(ob1)+50>getLeft(ob2)) && (getLeft(ob1)<getLeft(ob2)+50) && (getTop(ob1)+50>getTop(ob2)) && (getTop(ob1)<getTop(ob2)+50));}`	We need to make some adjustments from the Rock Storm game. This time, one of the objects is much smaller so we need to change the 100 to 50.

MOVING AT AN ANGLE

When we are coding in JavaScript, it is quite simple to move an object left and right or up and down. All we need to do is make sure it has its position property set to **absolute**, then change the left (**x** co-ordinates) and top (**y** co-ordinates) style values. To make it move at an angle, we need to use some more complex maths. Don't worry if you don't understand it all, but try to work out which parts of the following lines of code make it move so you can adapt it to use in other games you make.

If the submarine is travelling down at 30 degrees, then its motion can be broken down into how much it moves down and how much it moves to the right.

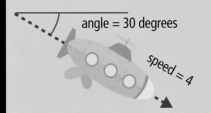

angle = 30 degrees

speed = 4

By using the maths functions **sine** and **cosine** we can turn movement at an angle into a combination of horizontal and vertical movements. In JavaScript, we type these as **Math.sin** and **Math.cos**:

Change **subX** by **speed** multiplied by the cosine of the sub's angle.

subX=subX+speed*Math.cos(Math.PI*angle/180);

subY=subY+speed*Math.sin(Math.PI*angle/180);

Change **subY** by **speed** multiplied by the sine of the sub's angle.

STEP 8 – MOVE THINGS

⇨ Each time the timer calls the function, we need to move the submarine and the coin. This function also calls another function **checkHit**, which tests to see if the sub has grabbed a coin. Finally, we check to see if the coin has got all the way to the bottom of the sea.

```
18 function moveThings(){
19     subX=subX+speed*Math.cos(Math.PI*angle/180);
20     subY=subY+speed*Math.sin(Math.PI*angle/180);
21     if(subX<-100){subX=innerWidth;}
22     if(subX>innerWidth){subX=-100;}
23     if(subY<-100){subY=innerHeight;}
24     if(subY>innerHeight){subY=-100;}
25     setLeft("sub",subX);
26     setTop("sub",subY);
27     y=getTop("coin");
28     setTop("coin", y+1+score*0.1);
29     checkHit();
30     if(y>window.innerHeight){gameOver();}
31 }
```

Change the variables subX and subY according to the sub's angle.

If the sub has gone past the left edge of the screen, move it to the right.

If it has gone too far right, move it all the way to the left hand side.

Move it to the bottom if it has gone too high.

Move it to the top if it has gone too low.

We need to move the submarine now we have worked out its new co-ordinates.

Find out where the coin is and store it in the variable **y**.

Move the coin down, getting faster as the score increases.

Call the function that will check if they have collided.

Add the code to end the game if the coin has gone past the bottom edge of the screen.

STEP 9 – DIRECT HIT?

⇨ This function checks to see if the sub has grabbed a coin, by testing to see if they are overlapping. If they are, the score goes up, the coin moves back to the top and a sound effect is played.

```
32  function checkHit(){
33    if(isOverlapping("sub","coin")){
34      score++;
35      document.getElementById("scoreTB").innerHTML="Score: "+score;
36      setTop("coin",0);
37      setLeft("coin",randomNumber(0,innerWidth-100));
38      new Audio("beep.mp3").play();
39    }
40  }
```

Test to see if the submarine is overlapping the coin. If it is, run the following code:

Increase the score by 1.

Move the coin back to the top of the screen.

Set a new random left position for the the coin.

Play the sound effect. Make sure the filename you type between the quotes matches the mp3 file you downloaded in step 3.

End the IF statement.

STEP 10 – STEER THE SUB

⇨ Type in the function below to handle the key press event. It changes the angle variable and also rotates the image.

```
41  function handleKeys(e){
42    if(e.keyCode==38){angle=angle-10;}
43    if(e.keyCode==40){angle=angle+10;}
44    document.getElementById("sub").style.
      webkitTransform = 'rotate('+angle+'deg)';
45  }
```

Reduce the angle variable by 10 degrees, if the code for the **up** arrow key has been sent.

Increase the angle variable by 10 degrees, if the code for the **down** arrow key has been sent.

Change the angle the image is shown at, to match the angle variable.

STEP 11 – GAME OVER

⇨ If one of the coins gets to the bottom of the sea, the following function will need to run:

```
46  function gameOver(){
47    clearInterval(gameTimer);
48    if(confirm("Game Over - Click OK to play again.")==true){
49      location.reload();
50    }
51  }
52  </script>
53  </html>
```

Stop the timer running to stop the objects moving.

Show a message asking the player if they want to play again? If they click OK, run the next line.

Reload the page and make the game start again.

End the IF statment

End the function.

End the script.

End the HTML.

 Save your file, reload the browser, then play!

THE COMPLETE CODE

```
1    <html>
2    <body style="background-color:#2980b9">
3        <img id="sub" style="position:absolute; top:500px; width:100px;" src="sub.png">
4        <img id="coin" style="position:absolute; left:300px; width: 50px;" src="coin.png">
5        <p id="scoreTB" style="position:absolute; color:white; font-size:20px; font-family:Arial;">Score: 0</p>
6    </body>
7    <script>
8        var score=0, angle=0, speed=4, gameTimer, subX=0, subY=500;
9        onkeydown=handleKeys;
10       gameTimer=window.setInterval(moveThings, 20);
11       function setLeft(id,x){document.getElementById(id).style.left=x+"px";}
12       function setTop(id,y){document.getElementById(id).style.top=y+"px";}
13       function getLeft(id){return document.getElementById(id).offsetLeft;}
14       function getTop(id){return document.getElementById(id).offsetTop;}
15       function randomNumber(low,hi){return(Math.floor(low+Math.random()*(1+hi-low)));}
16       function isOverlapping(ob1, ob2){
17           return ((getLeft(ob1)+50>getLeft(ob2)) && (getLeft(ob1)<getLeft(ob2)+50) &&
(getTop(ob1)+50>getTop(ob2)) && (getTop(ob1)<getTop(ob2)+50));}
18       function moveThings(){
19           subX=subX+speed*Math.cos(Math.PI*angle/180);
20           subY=subY+speed*Math.sin(Math.PI*angle/180);
21           if(subX<-100){subX=innerWidth;}
22           if(subX>innerWidth){subX=-100;}
23           if(subY<-100){subY=innerHeight;}
24           if(subY>innerHeight){subY=-100;}
25           setLeft("sub",subX);
26           setTop("sub",subY);
27           y=getTop("coin");
28           setTop("coin", y+1+score*0.1);
29           checkHit();
30           if(y>window.innerHeight){gameOver();}
31       }
32       function checkHit(){
33           if(isOverlapping("sub","coin")){
34               score++;
35               document.getElementById("scoreTB").innerHTML="Score: "+score;
36               setTop("coin",0);
37               setLeft("coin",randomNumber(0,innerWidth-100));
38               new Audio("beep.mp3").play();
39           }
40       }
41       function handleKeys(e){
42           if(e.keyCode==38){angle=angle-10;}
43           if(e.keyCode==40){angle=angle+10;}
44           document.getElementById("sub").style.webkitTransform = 'rotate('+angle+'deg)';
45       }
46       function gameOver(){
47           clearInterval(gameTimer);
48           if(confirm("Game Over - Click OK to play again.")==true){
49               location.reload();
50           }
51       }
52   </script>
53   </html>
```

› GLOSSARY

ANIMATION Making objects in your program move around.

BROWSER A program used to view web pages, such as Chrome or Internet Explorer.

BUG An error in a program that stops it working properly.

DEBUG To remove bugs (or errors) from a program.

ELEMENT One of the objects making up a web page, such as a paragraph or image.

EVENT Something that happens while the program is running, such as a mouse click or key press.

FUNCTION A reusable section of code combining a number of commands.

HTML (HYPERTEXT MARKUP LANGUAGE) The language used to build web pages.

JAVASCRIPT A programming language used to make web pages interactive or to build simple games.

OVERLAPPING When objects have collided but are not in exactly the same position.

PIXEL A small dot on the screen, can be used as a unit of measurement.

PROPERTY Information about the style of an element, such as its colour or size.

RANDOM NUMBER A number picked by the computer that can't be predicted.

TAGS Special words in an HTML document, surrounded by angle brackets <> defining an element.

TEXT EDITOR A program used to create and change code.

TIMER An object that runs a function after a specified delay, or at a regular interval.

TWO DIMENSIONAL ARRAY A list of lists used to represent a grid or table of data.

VARIABLE A value used to store information in a program that can change.

BUGS & DEBUGGING

When you find your code isn't working as expected, stop and look through each line of code you have put in. Here are some things to check:

🐛 Check you have spelt the commands correctly.

🐛 Check you have used the correct case (capitals and lower case).

🐛 Check you haven't missed any quotes.

🐛 Check you have closed tags correctly.

🐛 If images aren't showing, check filenames have been typed accurately.

🐛 If images aren't moving, check you have set position:absolute.

🐛 Make sure you have used the correct style of brackets and other symbols.

> COMMAND LIST

JAVASCRIPT COMMANDS

alert("Hello"); – shows "Hello" as a message in a pop up box.

var score=0; – defines a variable called score.

var gameTimer=window.setInterval(myFunction, 1000); – runs a function called **myFunction** every second.

clearInterval(gameTimer); – stops the timer called **gameTimer**.

function gameOver(); – defines a function called **gameOver()**.

document.getElementById("dog") – selects an element on the page.

Math.random() – creates a random number between 0 and 1.

Math.round() – rounds a decimal to the nearest whole number.

location.reload(); – reloads a page to restart the JavaScript (and the game).

HTML ELEMENTS

<html>...</html> – starts and ends the HTML file.

<script>...</script> – starts and ends the script section.

<img> – tags an image, such as a photo or piece of clipart.

<p>...</p> – tags a paragraph or line of text.

<body>...</body> – starts and ends the main body of the page, effectively the background of your program.

EVENTS

onclick – the mouse has been clicked.

onmousedown – the mouse has been pressed down (happens before click and mouse up).

onmouseup – the mouse button has been released.

onkeydown – a key has been pressed on the keyboard.

TIPS TO REDUCE BUGS

🐛 If you are making your own web page, spend time planning it before you start.

🐛 Practise debugging! Make a very simple web page and get a friend to change one line of code while you're not looking. Can you fix it?

🐛 When things are working properly, spend time looking through your code so you understand each line. To be good at debugging, you need to understand what each line of your code does and how your code works.

STYLE PROPERTIES

position:absolute – allows an element to be moved around by changing left and top properties.

left – sets how far across the screen an element (such as an image) is.

top – sets how far down from the top of the screen an element is.

height – sets the height of an element, such as an image (eg 20px means 20 pixels high).

width – sets the width of an element, such as an image.

-webkit-transition – sets how quickly an element changes its properties.

INDEX

First published in Great Britain in 2017 by Wayland

Text copyright © ICT Apps Ltd, 2017
Art and design copyright © Hodder and Stoughton Limited, 2017

All rights reserved.

Editor: Catherine Brereton
Freelance editor: Hayley Fairhead
Designer: Peter Clayman
Illustrator: Maria Cox

ISBN: 978 1 5263 0110 9
10 9 8 7 6 5 4 3 2 1

Wayland
An imprint of
Hachette Children's Group
Part of Hodder & Stoughton
Carmelite House
50 Victoria Embankment
London EC4Y 0DZ

An Hachette UK Company
www.hachette.co.uk
www.hachettechildrens.co.uk

Printed in China

The website addresses (URLs) included in this book were valid at the time of going to press. However, it is possible that contents or addresses may have changed since the publication of this book. No responsibility for any such changes can be accepted by either the author or the Publisher.

E-safety
Children will need access to the internet for most of the activities in this book. Parents or teachers should supervise this and discuss staying safe online with children.